Super Pred...

ORCA
Killer Whale

TJ Rob

Super-Predators: Orca Killer Whale
By TJ Rob

Published by:

TJ Rob

Suite 609

440-10816 Macleod Trail SE

Calgary, AB T2J 5N8 www.TJRob.com

ISBN 978-1-988695-56-3

TABLE OF CONTENTS

What are ORCAS?

Orcas are the largest of the Dolphin family, and one of the world's most powerful predators.

Orcas are marine mammals. As mammals, they have warm blood and nurse their calves with milk from the mothers. Orcas belong to the Cetacea class of sea mammals that includes Dolphins, Porpoises and Whales. Cetaceans are meat eaters (carnivorous) and have fins.

An Orca can also be called a Killer Whale, Blackfish or Seawolf.

Orcas are apex predators, as there are no animals that prey on them.

Why Killer Whales?

For centuries Orcas have been feared by mankind. Ancient sailors observed groups of Orcas hunting and preying on larger Whales. They called them "whale killers" - the term was flipped around to "Killer Whale", which we use today.

Their Latin name is "Orcinus Orca" - Orcinus means "of the kingdom of the dead", referring to Orcas deadly hunting abilities. The name Orca is a kind of Whale in Latin. The name Orca has also been thought to be a large round pot or jar - referring to the shape of the Orca.

Blue color indicates
where Orcas live.

White color indicates
areas with no Orcas

Orcas are found in all
of Earth's oceans.

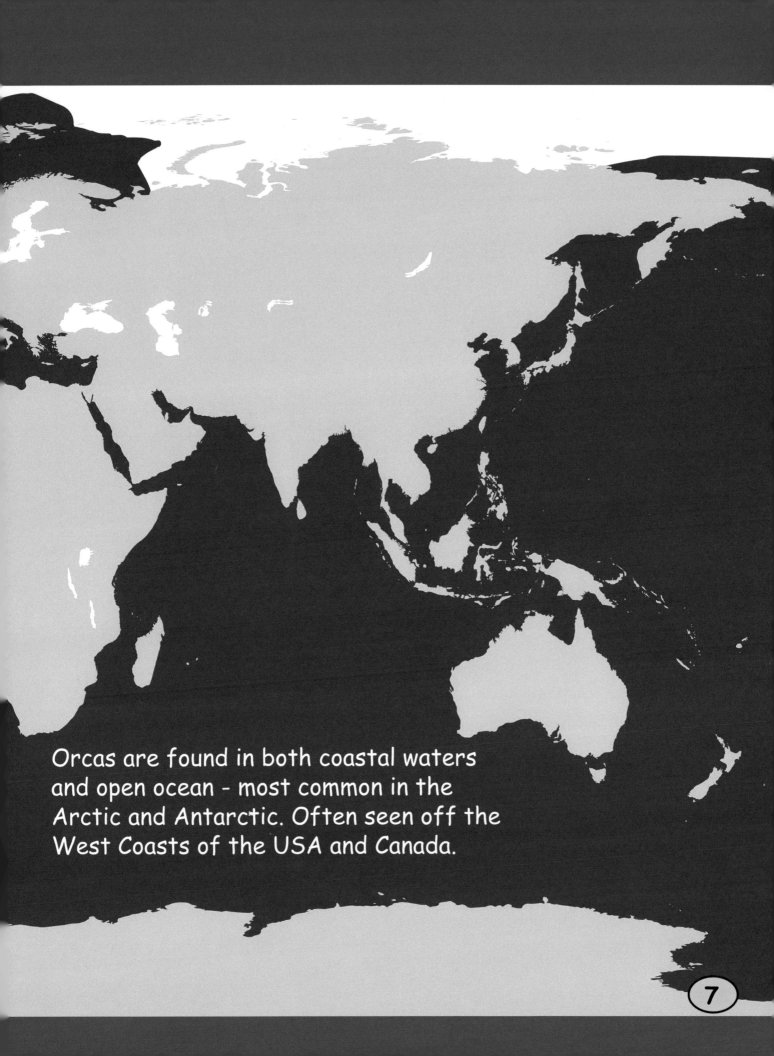

Orcas are found in both coastal waters and open ocean - most common in the Arctic and Antarctic. Often seen off the West Coasts of the USA and Canada.

How many Orcas are left in the wild?

Because Orcas are so widespread in all the oceans, it has been difficult to count exactly how many there are in the wild. There are no official estimates of the numbers of Orcas.

Amongst mammals, Orcas are only second to humans in their spread across our planet.

Scientists best estimates are that there are at least 50,000 Orcas in our oceans. Some Scientists believe that the number could be higher than 100,000 - no one knows for sure.

Orcas are not on the list of endangered animals.

Orcas in the wild

How big is an Orca?

Orcas are huge. Orcas are more than 100 times larger than humans.

Male Orcas are larger and heavier than females. Males can weigh up to 22,000 pounds (10,000 kg) and females can weigh up to 16,500 pounds (7,500 kg).

Males can reach up to 32 feet (10 m) long.
Female Orcas can reach 28 feet (8.5 m) long.

Size Comparison - an Orca VS a Human

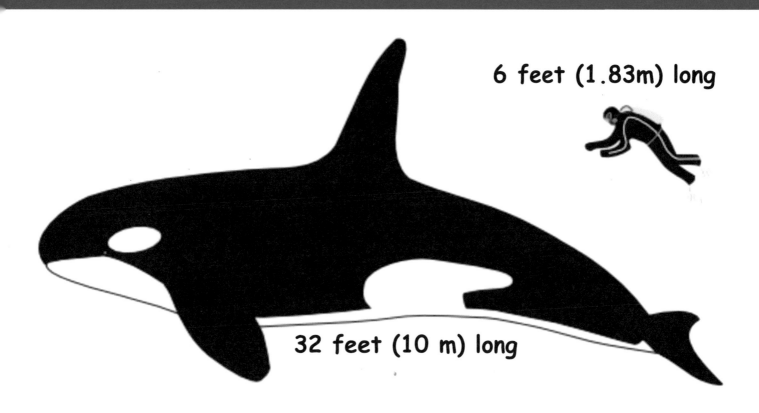

6 feet (1.83m) long

32 feet (10 m) long

Different Types of Orcas

Over the last 30 years researchers discovered more about wild Orcas than ever before. Scientists now know there are different subspecies of Orcas worldwide.

Each subspecies has different dietary needs, behavior patterns, social structures and habitat preferences.

Each Orca community uses different sounds to communicate with each other.

There are 10 different types of Orcas - 5 in the Northern Hemisphere, and 5 in the Southern Hemisphere:

Northern Hemisphere Subspecies:

   i. Resident Killer Whale
   ii. Biggs / Transient Killer Whale
   iii. Offshore Killer Whale
   iv. Eastern North Atlantic Type 1
   v. Eastern North Atlantic Type 2

Southern Hemisphere Subspecies:

   i. Atlantic Killer Whale - Type A
   ii. Pack Ice Killer Whale - Large Type B
   iii. Gerlache Killer Whale - Small Type B
   iv. Ross Sea Killer Whale - Type C
   v. Subantarctic Killer Whale - Type D

Pods and Clans

Orca groups are divided into pods and clans.

Orcas are highly social animals that travel and hunt in family groups called pods. Pods are made up of 5 to 30 Orcas, although some pods may join together to form a group of 100 or more. Pods are led by females.

Orcas use a complex form of communication with each other using different sounds. These sounds are a kind of language.

Each pod speaks the same language, but each pod has its own accent. It is like English speakers having an American, Australian or British accent.

A single clan is comprised of several pods all speaking the same language but with different accents.

Different clans speak completely different languages. When different clans come together for a chat this would be would be like an English speaker, Russian speaker and Chinese speaker trying to have a conversation.

A Pod of Orca swimming together

How long do Orcas live?

The average life expectancy of Orcas is over 50 years.

In some cases, they can reach up to 80 or even 90 years in the wild.

This is similar to Human life spans.

Orcas in captivity are a whole different matter. On average, in captivity they live for less than 10 years.

Hunting

Orcas use many different techniques to catch prey. They are very smart and skilled hunters.

One method is to slap their tails onto the water's surface, causing a wave to wash prey, such as Penguins or Sea Lions, off ice flows and into the water.

Norwegian Orcas hunt together in their pods. They herd small fish together into a tight ball close to the surface. Then the Orcas stun the fishes with their tail flukes and eat the stunned fish.

In the Antarctic, Orcas slide out onto ice flows to hunt Penguins. Orcas slide up onto sand bars or beaches to hunt Sea Lions. Orcas sometimes hit ice flows from below to knock their prey into the water.

Catching a Penguin

14

Chasing a Seal

Orcas are smart enough to follow commercial fishing boats. They eat fish that slip from the nets and fish thrown away by fishermen. In some areas, Orcas gather around longline boats and feed on the hooked fish.

Orcas do not seem to be afraid of any animal, no matter how ferocious they may be. Orcas will attack all kinds of Sharks, even Great Whites, and eat them.

Orcas are not afraid of size either. They have been seen attacking Blue Whales, the largest creatures on Earth. A pod of Orcas may attack a Blue Whale from several directions all at the same time.

Orcas also hunt individually. After a successful kill they share their fish with family members and their young.

What do Orcas like to Eat?

Orcas are not fussy eaters.

Orcas have also been reported to eat many types of animals including Sea Turtles, Dugongs, Moose, Penguins, Seabirds, Sharks, Whales, Seals, Porpoises, Sea Lions, Stingrays and of course many varieties of Fish.

Worldwide, Orcas have been observed preying on more than 140 species of animals including 50 different species of marine mammals.

The diet of Orcas depends on what part of the Earth's oceans they live in, and what is available there.

Dwarf Minke Whale

Sea Lion

Mako Shark

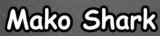

Harbor Seal

How much do Orcas eat?

Adult Orcas eat approximately 1% to 3.5% of their body weight in food every day. That would be between 220 pounds and 770 pounds (100 to 350 Kg) of food per day.

That's the equivalent amount of food that over 100 Americans eat in a single day!

Growing calves eat as much as 10% of their body weight during growth periods.

Orcas don't chew their food. They swallow their food whole, or they may tear or shred it.

Coming right at you!

Orca Communication

Orcas depend heavily on underwater sound for hunting, communication and to know where they are.

Orcas produce different types of sounds such as clicks, whistles and calls.

Whistles and calls are used for communication between animals in the pod.

Calls are the most common type of communication between Orcas. Calls sound like squeaks, screams, and squawks to us Humans.

An Orca Pod

Each pod has its own unique calls which are learned and used by those individuals. Calves are most likely to copy calls from their mothers. These unique calls within a pod are used to keep the group together.

When levels of noise are high, Orcas will increase the volume of their calls.

Echolocation

Orcas use special structures in their heads to send high frequency clicking sounds out into the water. These sounds travel through the water and bounce back off an object of interest.

The vibrations return to the Orca with valuable information that will give them accurate details about the object, mostly prey.

This process is called Echolocation. Echolocation works using sonar. This is the same way that submarines are able to "see" underwater.

Using Echolocation an Orca can find out about the size of the prey, how far away it is, how deep the water is and if there are any other predators nearby.

Once an Orca collects this information, it can decide to hunt that prey or look for another possible animal to hunt.

Bouncing sound off prey

Receiving an echo back

Cool ORCA Facts:

1. Orcas are the only natural predators of Great White Sharks.

2. Orcas can travel 100 miles (160 km) in a single day.

3. Newborn Orca calves can swim within 30 minutes of being born.

4. The oldest known Orca lived to 103 years old.

5. The brain of an Orca can weigh 15 to 17.5 pounds (7 to 8 kg) - 5 times more than a Human brain.

6. NO Orca has killed or seriously injured a Human being in the wild. All instances of injury or death to Humans were by Orcas in captivity.

7. Orcas in captivity become emotionally stressed and can even show signs of mental illness. This does not happen in the wild.

Orca Senses

HEARING

Orcas have very good hearing, particularly for listening underwater. They are also able to hear sounds both above and below the sound frequency range that Humans can hear.

An Orca's brain and nervous system can detect sounds at much higher speeds than humans. So they don't just hear better than us, but faster too!

SMELL

Orcas have no sense of smell. Most of their time is spent underwater - so a sense of smell would be used very little.

TASTE

In captivity, Orcas prefer specific types of fishes to others. Overall, we know very little about an Orca's sense of taste.

Orca Senses

SIGHT

The Orca has a highly developed sense of sight, both inside and outside of the water.

Their eyes are found at each side of the head, just behind and above the mouth. They are almost the same size as a Bull's eyes.
The lens of the eye in marine mammals is different from that of land mammals. It is more similar to the lens of a fish's eye than the lens of a land mammal's eye.

Glands close to the eyes, secrete an oily mucus, like a jelly, that lubricates and cleans the eyes while the Orca swims. This secretion helps protect the eye from infections and organisms that may harm the eye.

An Orca underwater

Orca Teeth

Big Teeth!

Orca teeth are cone shaped and interlocking. They have teeth on both the upper and lower jaws. Their teeth are blunt at the tip. Orcas use their teeth for biting and holding prey and are not designed for chewing.

They only have one set of teeth which are not replaced once lost. The number of teeth varies among individuals. There are usually 40 to 56 teeth in total. Most Orcas have 48 teeth.

Teeth are about 4 inches (10.15 cm) long and about 1 inch (2.5 cm) around.

Orcas get their teeth when they are about 3 weeks to 11 weeks of age. This is about the same time that calves start taking solid food from their mothers.

Teeth can get worn down in older individuals. Adult Offshore Orcas in the Northeast Pacific have highly worn teeth, likely caused by eating Sharks that have skin like sandpaper.

Body Parts of an Orca

SKIN

The skin of an Orca is smooth. The outer skin layer continually and rapidly renews itself, and the old skin sloughs off like dead skin in Humans.

A smooth body surface reduces drag in in the water, making swimming easier for the Orca.

BLUBBER

Beneath the outer skin layer, is a 3 to 4 inch (10 cm) thick layer of Blubber. Blubber is a layer of fat.

Blubber has two important functions:
1. It stores fat, which provides energy when food is in short supply.
2. Blubber reduces heat loss, which is important for regulating body Temperature. It helps insulate the Orca from the cold.

Smooth Skin reduces drag

DORSAL FIN

The dorsal fin is made of dense, fibrous connective tissue, without bones or cartilage.

Dorsal fin sizes and shapes are different for each Orca subspecies.

The dorsal fin of a male Orca is shaped like a triangle and is larger than that of a female. In adult males, it can reach a height of up to 6 feet (1.8 m) tall. In most females, the dorsal fin is slightly backward-curving and smaller - about 3 to 4 feet (0.9 to 1.2 m) tall.

The dorsal fin may help stabilize an Orca as it swims at high speeds, but it is not necessary for the Orca to keep its balance.

Dorsal Fin

Tail Flukes

FLUKES

Every Orca has a two-lobed tail. Each lobe is called a fluke. Flukes are flat pads of tough tissue, completely without bone or cartilage.

A large male Orca may have tail flukes measuring 9 feet (2.75 m) from tip to tip.

Long muscles in the back one-third of the body (above and below the spine) move the flukes up and down, which moves the Orca forward.

Body Parts of an Orca

PECTORAL FLIPPERS

Orcas use their rounded, paddle-like pectoral flippers to steer and to stop.

Pectoral flippers do have skeletal bones, just like the front limbs of land mammals, but they are much shorter.

Blood circulation in the pectoral flippers adjusts to help keep body temperature stable.

The pectoral flippers of male Orcas are larger than those of females. A large male Orca can have pectoral flippers as large as 6.5 feet (2 m) long and 4 feet (1.2 m) wide.

Huge Pectoral Flippers

BLOWHOLE

Orcas have a single blowhole on top of the head. An Orca breathes through its blowhole.

The blowhole is covered by a flap made of muscle. The flap provides a water-tight seal. To open its blowhole, an Orca contracts the muscular flap. The blowhole is relaxed in a closed position.

Blowhole

EARS

Ears are small hidden dimples just behind each eye. Orcas do not have any external ears with skin flaps, like other animals or humans.

Orca Babies

Orca babies are called calves. Calves are born throughout the year.

A female Orca will give birth every 3 to 10 years, to just 1 calf. The gestation period usually lasts for around 17 months. Almost half of all the calves die within their first year.

Calves are born in the water. Most births are tail-first, but head-first births have been seen.

Orca mother and calf

Calves are about 8.5 feet (2.6 m) long and 265 to 353 pounds (120 to 160 kg) at birth. Calves nurse for 5 to 10 seconds at a time, several times an hour. This goes on day and night until the calf has grown big enough to eat on its own.

Orca milk is very rich in fat. The fat content of Orca milk fluctuates as the calf develops. High-fat milk allows the calves to quickly build a thick layer of blubber.

Weaning begins at about 12 months and completes by the age of 2. All male and female pod members take care of the young.

When Orcas are born, their dorsal fin is flexible, but it stiffens as the calf gets older.

A mother Orca stays close to her newborn calf. Calves receive discipline from their mothers and other adults in the pod. Discipline can be in the form of restraining the calf (corralling the calf) or scratching the calf with their teeth.

Female Orcas start breeding at about 14 to 15 years of age. Females only breed for about 25 years then stop when they are about 40 years old. Each female only produces about 4 to 6 calves in her life.

To avoid inbreeding, males mate with females from other pods.
Males do not start to reproduce until they are about age 21.

Orca mother and calf

How fast do Ocrcas swim?

Orcas are among the fastest marine mammals, able to reach speeds in excess of 35 miles per hour (56 km/h) for short distances.

Most of the time Orcas cruise at much slower speeds, less than 8 miles per hour (13 km/h). They can cruise for long periods of time.

Orcas are very agile and maneuverable. Their smooth skins and blubber that give the Orca its shape, allows Orcas to be energy efficient when swimming.

Orcas cruising

An Orca porpoising

Orcas sometimes "porpoise" at the surface: they swim fast enough to break free of the water, gliding on the surface for a brief moment and then back into the water. Porpoising uses less energy than swimming in the water.

Wave-riding also saves energy. Orcas also ride ocean waves or the wake made by a boat. When riding a wave or a wake, Orcas can move twice as fast using the same energy.

A calf will swim close to its mother and can be carried in the mother's "slip stream". This helps the calf swim with less energy. It also allows the mother and the calf to keep up with the rest of the pod.

Diving - How Deep? How Long?

Although not generally deep divers, Orcas can dive deep. Normally Orcas spend most of their time in the top 65 feet (20 m) of the water. Most dives are less than this depth.

Adult male Orcas dive more often and deeper than adult females.

The deepest dive known for an Orca was 850 feet (259 m).

Orcas usually have a diving pattern where they take a few shallow dives of less than 1 minute, followed by a deeper dive where they stay under water longer.

They will generally surface to breathe after 3 to 5 minutes on these deeper dives, but can hold their breath for up to 15 minutes or more.

Diving

Do Orcas sleep?

Like other Dolphins, Orcas cannot go to sleep completely. They have to go up to the surface to breathe. Instead, they sleep with just half of their brains.

If an Orca's left eye is open, that means the right side of its brain is awake and the left side is asleep. If an Orca's right eye is open, that means the left side of its brain is awake and the right side is asleep.

When 1 half of the brain goes into a sleep state, the other half is able to see and hear and remains aware of its surroundings. The side that is awake also allows the animal to come to the surface of the water to breathe.

Orcas sleep at different times throughout the day and night, sometimes for short periods of time or for as long as 8 hours straight. Orcas often rest in a group, lined up alongside each other.

Newborn Orca calves and their mothers do not sleep at all for the first month of the calf's life. Over the next few months, the Orca calves gradually increase the amount of time they spend resting until they reach adult levels of sleep. Staying active and awake after birth may be a way to avoid predators and to maintain body temperature until the calf is big enough and has built up a layer of blubber.

Orca habits and behaviors

Researchers have noticed and named certain Orca behaviors.

BREACH - An Orca jumps out of the water and lands on the surface - usually on its side or on its back - with a huge splash. Sometimes the same Orca will breach several times in a row.

An Orca Breach

DORSAL FIN SLAPPING - The Orca rolls from one side to the other and slaps its fin on the surface of the water.

PEC-SLAPPING - An Orca slaps its pectoral flippers on the surface of the water - making loud sounds above and under the water.

SPYHOP - An Orca rises out of the water like it's standing on its tail, exposing its head - to have a look around.

LOB-TAILING - An Orca slaps its tail flukes on the surface of the water.

Spyhopping

Lob-Tailing

RUBBING BEACHES - Some Orcas off the Canadian British Columbia coast rub their bodies along the pebbly bottoms of shallow bays. They may do this to help remove dead skin.

Studies have shown that Orca are very curious. They love to "play" and manipulate objects.

How smart are Orcas?

Orcas kept in captivity have shown us how intelligent they are. They are very smart animals.

Orcas can understand hand signals, voice commands and symbols on flashcards. They even have some understanding of numbers.

Orcas have fantastic memories. In tests conducted with Orcas in captivity, they could remember tests up to 25 years after they were conducted.

Tests done on Orcas in captivity show that they can recognize themselves in mirrors.

Orcas communicate often and sometimes across great distances.

They teach language and lessons to their young. Orcas have different hunting techniques which they pass down from generation to generation.

They understand fun, since they have been observed playing with food. Orcas are capable of understanding other emotions too.

Orcas are very curious and are great problem solvers. Orcas have a basic understanding of physics since they are known to create waves of water to knock prey off of a bit of ice. They have learnt how to steal fish off long line fishing boats, including avoiding decoys and other measures designed to stop them.

HUMAN THREATS

Commercial-Hunting

Orcas are still hunted in Japan, Greenland, Indonesia and some parts of the Caribbean. They are killed for their fat, skin, flesh and internal organs.

Capture for Entertainment

Orcas intelligence makes them attractive to Humans, as they are able to learn to perform aerobatics. Live catches of Orcas are sometimes made for displaying them in aquariums and animal parks.

Habitat Pollution

Water pollution directly affects Orcas health. For example, in the coastal waters of British Columbia (Canada), the presence of chemicals is so high that it is a risk for Orcas. Oil spills are very dangerous to Orcas. Oil directly damages their bodies. Also, oil spills decrease the numbers of Orca prey.

Excessive Noise

Orcas are very sensitive to noise since they use Echolocation. Military and industrial activities that generate excessive noise tend to disturb Orcas.

Decreased Prey

Habitat pollution as well as over-fishing, reduces the number of prey available to Orcas.

Collisions with Boats

Every year there is more ship traffic on the oceans. A collision with any boat can cause mild to severe wounds. The wounds have the potential to get infected and cause their death.

Problems with Fishermen

Many fishermen see Orcas as a threat because they have learned to steal the fish from their longlines. Although most fishermen use humane methods to chase away Orcas from their lines, some fishermen shoot Orcas to stop them from getting their catches.

Climate Change

Increases in the temperature, or in the water level, of the oceans is changing the availability of Orcas usual prey.

THANKS FOR READING!

Please leave a review at your favorite bookseller's website.
Share with other readers what you liked about this book.

Visit www.TJRob.com to learn about other exciting books by TJ Rob:

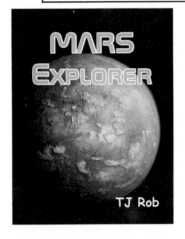

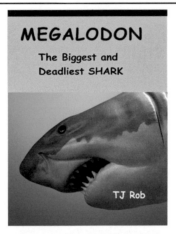

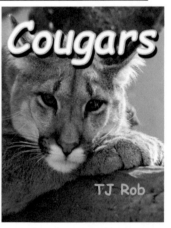

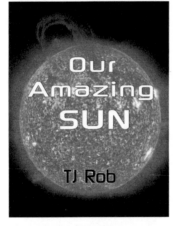

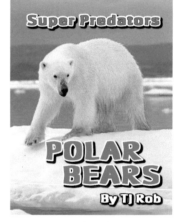

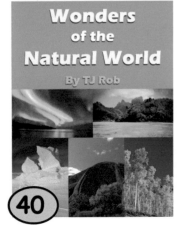

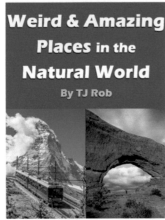

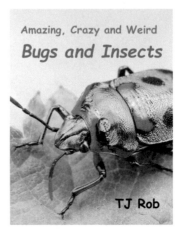

Made in United States
Troutdale, OR
12/07/2023

15469262R00026